ENDING THE MILITARY'S COUNTERNARCOTICS MISSION

Let this be recorded as the time when America rose up and said no to drugs. The scourge of drugs must be stopped. And I am asking tonight for an increase of almost a billion dollars in budget outlays to escalate the war against drugs. The war must be waged on all fronts. Our new drug czar, Bill Bennett, and I will be shoulder to shoulder in the executive branch leading the charge.... And much of [the money] will be used to protect our borders, with help from the Coast Guard and the Customs Service, the Departments of State and Justice, and, yes, the US military.[1]

—President George H. W. Bush
February 9, 1989

Thus, the US "War on Drugs" was introduced to the US public. The US military had worked with other countries combating illicit narcotics production and trafficking before that time. President Bush's February 1989 primetime speech, however, marked a shift that would lead to billions of taxpayer dollars being spent by the Department of Defense in its counternarcotics mission, named a national priority by then-President Bush and every US President since then. This paper will question the results of the US military's counternarcotics effort and propose that in today's constrained fiscal environment, perhaps the military should begin to withdraw from that mission and instead refocus its efforts on its key mission areas, i.e., more tangible threats to our nation's security.

Background

Prior to FY1989, DoD's counternarcotics efforts had been largely limited to supporting law enforcement agencies with training, assistance, and aircraft.[2] Giving the Department of Defense (DoD) an expanded counternarcotics mission had been a subject of some debate in 1988, when then-Secretary of Defense Frank Carlucci and former Secretary of Defense Caspar Weinberger publicly opposed formally expanding the US Armed Forces' role in narcotics interdiction. They argued "that the mission of the armed forces is to protect the nation from foreign armies, not drug smugglers, and that civilian law enforcement agencies, especially the Coast Guard, should be given the resources necessary to do the job."[3] Under new leadership, the Department of Defense (DoD) was forced to comply when the new President George H.W. Bush introduced the *National Drug Control Strategy* which brought the US military into the forefront of what was then called the "War on Drugs" in 1989.

> As the perceived threat of communism faded and eventually collapsed in the 1980s, the drug war replaced the Cold War as the military's central mission in the Western Hemisphere. Few in the military establishment, however, embraced the counternarcotics mission enthusiastically.[4]

National Security Directive (NSD) 18 identified "reducing the flow of illegal narcotic substances to the United States," as a principal foreign policy objective of the Bush Administration. The Directive stated that narcotics abuse is devastating to our society, has had a "destabilizing effect on friendly governments," and should be "dealt with aggressively."[5] The corresponding National Defense Authorization Act designated DoD as the lead agency for the "detection and monitoring of aerial and maritime transit of illegal drugs into the United States."[6] It directed Secretary of Defense Dick Cheney to revise DoD policy guidance to expand military support of US counternarcotics efforts and provide counternarcotics training to the governments of the Andean region, under what became the Andean Initiative.[7] The military's focus was and remains on illicit-narcotics eradication and interdiction.[8] Initial DoD guidance approved by Cheney included, "(1) Assistance for nation-building, (2) Operational support to host-country forces, and (3) Cooperation with host-country forces to prevent drug exports."[9] On September 18, 1989 Cheney called on the leaders of the armed forces to develop plans to counter the flow of illegal drugs from entering the US. He also called for plans to deploy military forces in support of US and allied law enforcement agencies, especially along the US' southwestern border. [10]

Since then, DoD has spent billions of dollars combating the illicit drug trade, with little to show for it. According to one British correspondent, "Four decades on, in a world (and an America) accursed by poverty and drugs, there is almost universal agreement that the war on drugs has failed as thoroughly as that on poverty."[11] There are several possible reasons for the low return on investment of the US military's counternarcotics efforts. One reason for this apparent failure is that the armed forces are not appropriately trained to combat criminals and criminal organizations. Another reason is that focusing on the supply side of the problem by combating the narcotics production and trafficking has proven ineffective over the decades DoD has been engaged in the effort. A third reason for the apparent failure of the military's counternarcotics program is a lack of viable metrics. Finally, a far more controversial reason relates to the nature of the illicit drug problem. If illegal drugs and the narcotics production and trafficking organizations are actually social welfare and law enforcement challenges, rather than threats to national security, the military is arguably the wrong tool to counter them.

The US Department of Defense (DoD) should begin to wind down its role in combating drug trafficking. The military has been visibly and formally engaged in the counternarcotics effort since 1989, when so directed by Congress and the President. In that time, its impact has been minimal, with little to no effect on either the supply or price of illicit narcotics entering the US. The mission was initially opposed by DoD leadership which subsequently was compelled to implement it. Especially in this era of fiscal austerity, the application of military force to a mission which arguably falls outside the military's key mission areas seems doubly inappropriate.

Mission Mismatch

The armed forces are primarily trained to fight other military or paramilitary forces, or as the saying goes, "to kill people and break things." Military personnel are not trained for law enforcement, and especially not for law enforcement activities on the US side of our borders where they are routinely called upon to provide direct support to law enforcement agencies (LEAs) against narcotics traffickers. One example is that military personnel are collocated with Drug Enforcement Agency (DEA) personnel at the El Paso Intelligence Center where they share intelligence information and support LEA operations.

One guiding principle of DoD's counternarcotics efforts is that in accordance with the Posse Comitatus Act of 1878, the military is not permitted to take an active role in law enforcement activities. Still, since 1980, Congress and the President have significantly weakened the prohibitions of the Posse Comitatus Act seemingly in order to permit military personnel to more aggressively pursue a counternarcotics border mission.[12] One example is the Military Cooperation with Civilian Law Enforcement Agencies Act, passed by the US Congress in 1981.[13] The Act, codified in Title 10 of the US Code, Chapter 18, allows the DoD to provide equipment, facilities, training, advice, and "any information collected during the normal course of military training or operations that may be relevant to a violation of any Federal or State law within the jurisdiction of such officials."[14] In the late 1980s, when increasing DoD's role in narcotics trafficking was under debate, Congress favored giving law enforcement duties to the military in patrolling the nation's borders. In 1988, the US House of Representatives voted to have the military "seal the borders" to narcotics trafficking within 45 days, "while the Senate

voted overwhelmingly to expand the role of the military in the anti-drug campaign."[15]

The 1989 National Defense Authorization Act, cited earlier, identified DoD as the single

lead agency for the tracking and monitoring of illicit drug transfers into the United

States, by sea or by air, also effectively weakening the provisions of the Posse

Comitatus Act.[16] Although given the narcotics trafficking detection and monitoring

mission in the air and at sea, DoD was not given responsibility for that mission on land.

Occasionally, the military has been called upon to provide surveillance and

monitoring support to law enforcement authorities along our southwestern land border,

at a significant expense. Two recent National Guard deployments to the border cost

about $1.35 billion through last September. The first was significantly larger with about

6,000 personnel, from June 2006 to July 2008. A deployment of some 1,200 personnel

from July 2010 through September 2011 cost close to $145 million. The deployments

were authorized under Title 32 of the US Code, and therefore, federally funded; but the

troops served under their respective governors.[17] In 2006, President George W. Bush

announced the deployment of up to 6,000 National Guard troops to the southern border

under Title 32 of the US Code. The Guard units also served under their respective

governors, while fully funded by the federal government, i.e., DoD.[18]

DoD rotary and fixed wing aircraft began replacing the National Guard contingent

in January of 2012. "Aircraft outfitted with high-tech radar and other gear can cover

more ground than troops in spotting and catching illegal border crossers and drug

smugglers," the Army Times reported.[19] In addition to surveillance activity, the aircraft

are also available to transport Customs and Border Patrol (CBP) agents to a site where illegal activity is spotted.[20] The National Guard planned to reduce its presence on the border from the 1,200 authorized in 2010 to 300 in 2011, and to none by the end of 2012. The premise is that CBP would, in that time, increase its number of agents on the border as well as the requisite technology.[21]

Some, such as pundit Bill O'Reilly of Fox News and Texas Governor Rick Perry, suggest raising the US military's role in the counternarcotics realm by again having its active duty component patrol our southern border with Mexico, or by increasing DoD's unmanned aerial vehicle monitoring of the border.[22] Perry even suggested during a campaign stop last October that he if were elected President, he might deploy US military forces to the Mexican side of the border. "It may require our military in Mexico working in concert with them [the Mexicans] to kill these drug cartels and keep them off our border."[23] US Senators John McCain and Jon Kyl in 2010 called for 3,000 National Guardsmen to be sent to the Arizona-Mexico border as part of a comprehensive national border security plan to "combat illegal immigration, drug and alien smuggling, and violent activity along the southwest border."[24] The presence of armed military personnel along our nation's borders would not present the image of a welcoming democratic country and could cause consternation in Mexico. More significantly, the Mexican government is trying to downplay the US' role, especially its military role, in assisting its law enforcement and military counternarcotics efforts. Also, Soldiers and Marines are not border guards, and are not trained for law enforcement responsibilities. The dangers of having them on the border can be seen in the 1997 shooting of 18-year-old Texas high school student Esequiel Hernandes, who was herding his family's goats near the Mexican border. Unfortunately for him, the teenager fired his .22 caliber rifle in the direction of a camouflaged Marine patrol, possibly to scare away wild dogs. Rather than announcing themselves and demanding that the teen drop his weapon, as law enforcement officers would have been compelled to do, one Marine returned fire, with deadly consequences. [25]

Supply and Demand

Attacking the "supply" side of the US drug problem has proven largely ineffective in that as long as "demand" persists, the suppliers have demonstrated they will rise to the challenge of providing what the market will bear. The premise of the US government's counternarcotics efforts is that by interfering with the supply of illegal drugs entering the US, and cutting into that supply, the laws of economics would dictate that prices would increase to a point where fewer people could and would purchase illegal substances. Toward that end, the US military trains and equips the armed forces and law enforcement agencies of other countries to combat narcotics producers and traffickers, detects and monitors drug trafficking, participates in drug eradication programs and shares information with US law enforcement entities and partner nations.[26] As of November 2011, DoD had active counternarcotics programs in the following 22 countries: Peru, Colombia, Afghanistan, Bolivia, Ecuador, Pakistan, Tajikistan, Turkmenistan, Uzbekistan, Azerbaijan, Kazakhstan, Kyrgyzstan, Armenia, Guatemala, Belize, Panama, Mexico, Dominican Republic, Guinea-Bissau, Senegal, El Salvador, and Honduras.[27]

More recently, the training of the Mexican Marines is one of several ways in which the US military has quietly escalated its role in Mexico's drug war in the past three years since implementation of the Merida Initiative, part of a US "Whole of Government" effort to support the Mexican Government's fight against the cartels. Under the initiative,

7

the US gave $900 million in assistance to Mexico from 2009 through 2011. It also shifted from a focus on equipping and funding the Mexicans, to training, thus enhancing partnership capabilities. The program has had numerous operational and tactical successes, with more than 30 senior cartel leaders having been arrested or killed, compared with one in the six years prior to Merida.[28] The long term effects of arresting or killing cartel leaders appear negligible, however, as others rise up to replace them (see the "hydra effect" below) or a cartel splits and two leaders replace the one, as was the case with the Beltran Leyva organization.[29] *The New York Times* similarly explains that, "the violence has been fueled in part by the splintering of drug organizations under siege, which led to escalating rounds of bloody infighting over territory and criminal rackets."[30] Meanwhile, the drug related violence in Mexico goes on unabated. According to Mexico's *Excelsior* newspaper, drug violence reportedly claimed 47,515 lives from December 2006, when President Felipe Calderon deployed thousands of troops against the cartels, through September 2011.[31] When that number of lost lives is divided by the number of corresponding months and days, an average of one person died every hour of every day during that period. When the data for the first nine months of 2011 is viewed separately, the rate of violence skyrocketed, with one person succumbing to drug violence every half-hour, or 48 killings per day.[32]

The rise of drug trafficking organizations in Mexico coincided with the US' success in training Colombia to combat its drug cartels. The US' Plan Colombia arguably contributed to Mexico's surge in violence by shifting Colombia's narcotics trafficking organizations and routes elsewhere. The Plan unintentionally pushed transshipment routes into West Africa for cocaine destined for Europe and Africa, and up through Mexico for cocaine intended for North America, greatly strengthening and even giving rise to some of Mexico's more powerful cartels.[33] An Associated Press report in 2009 observed, "The United States has spent hundreds of millions of dollars to help Colombia dismantle its major cartels but may have actually helped the Mexicans gain traction in South America in the process."[34] In fact, NSD 18 which outlined the International Counternarcotics Strategy in 1989, warned that successful counternarcotics efforts in Colombia could lead to a "shifting of trafficking organizations and infrastructure to locations in Bolivia and Peru, … without expanded efforts in those two countries."[35] The Directive therefore proposed counterdrug assistance to all three countries, but did not envision the subsequent shifting of trafficking patterns beyond the Andean countries.

The US Government effort has been predicated on the belief that a successful counternarcotics strategy should attack the supply side of the problem. A drop in supply would lead to higher narcotics prices which would drive many users out of the market. However, according to *Drug War Politics: The Price of Denial*, "the attempt to suppress the drug trade through a war on supply generates two self-defeating effects – the profit paradox and the hydra effect – which together doom the effort."[36] The profit paradox is created by cartels' raising prices to compensate for depleted supply. The higher prices mean higher profits, encouraging more suppliers to enter the market. More suppliers maintain or even raise the supply of drugs available, countering any pressure to raise prices. Therefore, law enforcement and military efforts to attack the supply side of the illicit narcotics problem has no noticeable effect on the price of product. The hydra effect simply asserts that if one source of an illegal drug is shut down another will take its place.[37] The same concept in counterterrorism is often referred to as "whack a mole."[38]

The result of the military's supply-side involvement is summarized by *The Oberver's* Ed

Vulliamy:

> The war in the so-called "producing" countries has ravaged Colombia, is currently tearing Mexico apart, and again threatens Afghanistan, Central America, Bolivia, Peru and Venezuela. In places such as West Africa, the war is creating "narco states" that have become effective puppets of the mafia cartels the war has spawned.[39]

Metrics

One factor significantly complicating assessing DoD's progress, and impeding

progress in the counternarcotics effort is the lack of a coherent system within the

Department to measure its effectiveness in combating illicit drug production and

trafficking. A 2010 report by the General Accounting Office (GAO) states that measuring

performance is essential in providing managers with a "basis for making fact-based

decisions, but that DoD's system is inadequate and the results not utilized to improve

management and oversight of the system."[40]

As cited above, the US Government position has been that been that success

could be somehow measured by a reduction in the amount of illegal drugs entering the

US, and a subsequent rise in the price of those drugs as a result of the reduced supply,

in accordance with the basic tenets of supply and demand. The 2011 *Department of*

Defense Counternarcotics and Global Threats Strategy dedicates a page to the

discussion of a need for "metrics" regarding the development of performance indicators

to "observe progress and measure actual versus expected results."[41] Such wording is

too vague to be of significant practical value in assessing accomplishments to date. The

Strategy identifies the importance of using performance metrics and states that the

Deputy Assistant Secretary of Defense for Counternarcotics and Global Threats (DASD

CN&GT) "with inputs from stakeholders, *will issue* guidance and instructions for formulating and reporting on performance metrics that reflect theater-level operational plan CN&GT objectives and activities."[42] In short, metrics guidance is forthcoming, some twenty-three years into the directed effort. When asked what metrics the DASD uses to judge the effectiveness of its counternarcotics programs, a senior DoD official observed that if using the decreased quantity and increased prices of illicit narcotics in the US as measures of effectiveness, the military's counternarcotics efforts could not be deemed successful.[43] The official did, however, cite some specific cases of DoD support resulting in major seizures. Nonetheless, despite more than two decades of concerted DoD effort, US law enforcement agencies have witnessed no significant drop in the supply nor rise in price of illegal narcotics entering the US.[44] According to the UN's *2011 World Drug Report,* the retail (street) price of heroin in the US in (adjusted for inflation) 2009 dollars dropped from $231 per gram in 1990 to $157 per gram in 2009, and when further adjusted for purity as well as inflation, dropped significantly further from $1,051 per gram in 1990 to less than half, at $491 in 2009.[45] Some of that price drop could be attributable to the relatively stable demand for heroin in the US; however, if rising prices for illicit drugs is considered a measure of effectiveness of the US' counternarcotics efforts, we appear to be falling short.

The UN estimates that the US comprises the single largest cocaine market in the world, accounting for the consumption of some 157 metric tons of the 440 metric tons available for consumption worldwide in 2009. That data point belies the fact that as compared with estimates for 1989, US cocaine consumption has dropped some 70%.[46] Whether the drop in domestic consumption is the result of changing preferences or successes in prevention is unclear; but there has been no corresponding increase in interdiction successes. In fact, interdictions along the southwest border area dropped from 27,361 kilograms of cocaine in FY2006 to 17,830 kilograms in FY2010, and from 69,561 across the entire US in FY2006 down to 44.063 kilograms in FY2010, as demonstrated by the below chart.[47] During the same period, seizures of methamphetamines and marijuana increased significantly.

TOTAL US** SEIZURES BY DRUG IN KILOGRAMS

REGION	FY2006	FY2007	FY2008	FY2009	FY2010
Cocaine					
Southwest Border Area*	27,361	24,780	17,459	18,737	17,830
Northern Border	2	<1	<1	18	23
Rest of US	42,198	33,177	28,547	29,629	26,210
Total US	69,561	57,957	46,006	48,384	44,063
Methamphetamine					
Southwest Border Area	2,706	2,128	2,221	3,278	4,486
Northern Border	<1	1	135	0	11
Rest of US	2,872	3,100	3,696	3,323	4,202
Total US	5,578	5,229	6,052	6,601	8,699
Heroin					
Southwest Border Area	449	358	496	737	905
Northern Border	5	<1	0	28	20
Rest of US	1,719	1,631	1,404	1,485	1,637
Total US	2,173	1,989	1,900	2,250	2,562
Marijuana					
Southwest Border Area	1,046,419	1,459,162	1,242,758	1,730,344	1,545,138
Northern Border	5,455	3,084	2,369	3,784	2,194
Rest of US	237,330	263,904	227,948	241,000	262,164
Total US	1,289,204	1,726,150	1,473,075	1,975,128	1,809,496

Source: National Drug Threat Assessment 2011[48]

*The Southwest Border Area includes seizures made by federal, state and local law enforcement officers along and within 150 miles of the border

Figure 1.

Statistics can raise more questions than they answer. There appears to be little data identifying or quantifying the role played by DoD in LEA tactical successes in intercepting illegal narcotics along the border. One may point to kilograms of narcotic X seized in a given year (as shown above); but DoD's role in those interdictions is unclear since DoD is not authorized to conduct US interdictions, only to support them.[49] DoD assists LEAs on our borders primarily with reconnaissance assets, "boots on the ground" (usually National Guard personnel under Title 32 authority) surveillance support, transportation assistance and information sharing. The *Army Times* reports that in fiscal year 2011, "apprehensions on the Southwestern border fell to 340,252, one-fifth the level reported in fiscal [year] 2000,...In Arizona, Border Patrol apprehensions fell to 129,118, the lowest number in 17 years."[50] A significant number these apprehensions were almost certainly drug-related; however, data breaking out the types of apprehensions conducted is not readily available. Without useful metrics, one is hard-pressed to demonstrate a consistent track record of DoD results in the counterdrug mission. Only the dollar cost of those efforts is readily quantifiable.

FY2005	FY2006	FY2007	FY2008	FY2009	FY2010	FY2011
$1,147.8	$936.1	$1,137	$1,314.8	$1,397.2	$1,558.3	$1,689.2[51]

Figure 2. DoD Counternarcotics Funding (in millions of US dollars)

Nature of the Threat

The flow of illegal drugs into the US is both a legal-criminal and a social welfare concern; but does it rise to the level of a national security threat that merits military involvement under the umbrella of homeland defense? Even the highest policy-making levels of the US Government seem to disagree. The *2010 National Security Strategy*

13

warns, "Transnational criminal threats and illicit trafficking networks continue to expand dramatically in size, scope, and influence – posing significant national security challenges for the United States and our partner countries."[52] One could argue over the semantics of what constitutes a "national security challenge" versus a "national security threat;" but suffice it say, a "challenge" usually does not rise to the level of a "threat." Meanwhile, among the five overarching policy objectives identified in the *US Strategy to Combat Transnational Organized Crime* (TOC), is:

> Defeat transnational criminal networks that pose the greatest threat to national security.... Further, we will seek to prevent collaboration between criminal and terrorist networks and deprive them of their critical resources and infrastructure, such as funding, logistical support for transportation, staging, procurement, safe havens for illicit activities, and the facilitation of services and materiel, which could include WMD material.[53]

Thus, the *US Strategy to Combat TOC*, above, states that transnational criminal networks may post a threat to national security. Meanwhile, the new *National Defense Strategy* (NDS), released in January, does not even mention DoD's counternarcotics mission.[54] Further, it defines the US military's role in homeland defense more narrowly than the US Government and DoD have in the past, explaining, "US forces will continue to defend US territory from direct attack by state and non-state actors."[55] The activities of drug trafficking organizations would hardly constitute a "direct attack" on US territory, probably not what was envisioned by the drafters of the NDS. The NDS also redefines Homeland Defense and Defense Support to Civil Authorities in way that precludes addressing counternarcotics.[56] The President's 2012 State of the Union address similarly defined homeland defense as responding to attacks directed against the US.[57] In his prepared statement for the Senate Select Committee on Intelligence on January 31, 2012, Director of National Intelligence James Clapper did not identify drug cartels or cartel violence in Mexico as a serious national security concern. Rather, he asserted that although the "Mexican cartels have a presence in the United States,…we are not likely to see the level of violence that is plaguing Mexico spill across the US border."[58] He also stated that, "the factor that drives most of the bloodshed in Mexico – competition for control of trafficking routes and networks of corrupt officials – is not widely applicable to the small retail drug trafficking activities on the US side of the border."[59]

A Mexican commentator recently observed that the Mexican government's efforts to combat the cartels with military force, with support of the US, only leads to more violence. He observed with some irony that the US then worries about the possible cross-border seepage of the resulting violence it does not realize it has caused.[60] The violence associated with Mexican narcotics trafficking organizations remains almost exclusively within Mexico's borders, despite some overflow into the US' southern border states. Drug-related violence within the US falls largely in the domain of drug dealers, drug users and gang members, i.e., criminals, and as such, does not easily fall into the category of a national security threat.

The term "narcoterrorism" was coined ostensibly to demonstrate the nexus between narcotics trafficking organizations and terrorist organizations. By effectively identifying cartels as terrorist organizations "by another name," one can more easily justify claims that that they threaten US national security interests. The term was likely coined to sound the national security alarm and obtain counterterrorism funding in the continuing effort to combat the drug cartels, according to one senior Defense official.[61] Further, referring to the business of cartels as constituting narcoterrorism, and formally identifying them as terrorist organizations would allow the US Government a range of strategy and policy options and military tools that would otherwise not be available in combating them.[62] While both drug cartels and terrorist organizations use violence as a tactic to further their goals, they are different. Cartels are criminal enterprises whose leaders are motivated by profit. "Mexican and Colombian drug trafficking organizations earn between $18 billion and $39 billion a year."[63] Terrorist organizations have a political, or perhaps, even a social or religious goal. Former Mexican Attorney General Arturo Chavez repeatedly maintained that the narcotics cartels were not terrorist organizations. He observed that their violence was not intended to weaken the state, and that their motivation was economic, not ideological.[64] Also referring to the Mexican cartels, Dr. Paul Kan observes that:

> Even violent acts by the cartels and gangs directed at government targets are meant as a signal for the government to retreat from its confrontational stance; they are designed to intimidate the government rather than to serve as a political statement...Terror and insurgent groups try to sway constituents with violence; cartels try to satisfy clients by circumventing or undermining the state."[65]

Some Members of the US Congress, most notably those from the southwestern border states, have even suggested that Mexican cartels be identified as terrorist organizations and placed on the State Department's Foreign Terrorist Organizations List.[66] In support of a Republican bill to do just that, the Enhanced Border Security Act (HR 3401), Representative Michael Paul of Texas stated, "I believe that the drug cartels are acting within the federal definition of terrorism, which basically says to intimidate a civilian population or government by extortion, kidnapping or assassination. That is precisely, precisely what the drug cartels do. They extort."[67] Representative Eliot Engel disagreed with the characterization, plainly stating that Mexico is experiencing "narco-crime" and not terrorism, observing:

> If I were living in a place where gun battles were leaving scores of people dead and previously safe streets were now hideouts for thugs and criminals, I would feel a sense of terror, too.... [however] There is a difference between acts which can cause terror and terrorist acts.... The narco-criminals in Mexico have no political aims, they are brutal outlaws who want money, but they don't want to throw out the government and take over."[68]

Representative Michael McCaul of Texas points to last year's failed plot by Iranian government agents who believed they were working with a Mexican Los Zetas cartel associate to assassinate the Saudi Ambassador to the US, to demonstrate alleged ties between drug cartels and terrorism.[69] The so-called cartel member was actually a paid informant of the US Drug Enforcement Administration (DEA).[70] The cartel did not support the Iranian effort. According to Robert Valencia, a Research Fellow with the Council on Hemispheric Affairs:

> having the US State Department label the Zetas a terrorist organization solves nothing. The addition of the Zetas to that list won't stop cartels from running the drug market nor from establishing international ties. Furthermore, unlike terrorist organizations such as al-Qaida, these cartels' goals do not include attacking the US. The Zeta cartel's motive is money, not ideology.[71]

The experience of Colombia is very different from that of Mexico. In Colombia, insurgent organizations such as the Revolutionary Armed Forces of Colombia (FARC), National Liberation Army (ELN), and the now disbanded Democratic Alliance (M-19), routinely funded their operations through activities including narcotics trafficking. In the 1980s the lines dividing the activities of the insurgent organizations and the cartels were sometimes blurred, as in the 1985 M-19 and drug cartel-coordinated attack on the Palace of Justice in Bogota, in which 115 people were killed, including 11 Supreme

17

Court justices.[72] A 2012 State Department report on Colombia explains that since the early 1980s, "left-wing guerrillas" have conducted "terrorist and drug-trafficking activities," while the drug cartels have continued their violence.[73] Thus, even though Colombia's insurgents have used trafficking to line their coffers and fund their operations, they are not to be confused with narcotics cartels. Also, cartel related violence has diminished since Colombian security forces killed notorious Medellin cartel leader Pablo Escobar in 1993.[74]

There undeniably is an occasional confluence of interests between drug cartels and terrorist organizations;[75] however, such a confluence does not make cartels terrorist organizations, nor does an occasional linkage confirm the existence of so-called narcoterrorism. Research on this connection is episodic and data is not readily available. Some disincentives for cartels and terrorist organizations partnering are:

> increased attention from government authorities; fear of compromising internal security; ideological resistance to illegal endeavors, such as drug trafficking, kidnapping and fraud; and sufficient sources of non-criminal funding from charities, large private donors, licit businesses and state sponsors.[76]

Recommendations and Conclusion

The US Government should focus on attacking the "demand" side of the illicit narcotics problem in the US. A fundamental principle of economics is that demand drives supply; therefore, demand for illicit drugs drives narcotics production and trafficking. Mexican President Felipe Calderón has repeatedly asked the United States to do more to address the demand side of the drug trade, as well as the flow of weapons from the US to the cartels.[77] Much of the cartels' market is in the US. Even the National Drug Control Strategy acknowledges that demand within our borders contributes significantly to the illicit drug trade:

We must begin our efforts to disrupt TOC [transnational organized crime] by looking inward and acknowledging the causes that emanate from within our own borders to fuel and empower TOC. The demand for illegal drugs within the United States fuels a significant share of the global drug trade, which is a primary funding source for TOC networks and a key source of revenue for some terrorist and insurgent networks.[78]

Illicit drugs endanger the public health and safety of our citizens. Resources should be directed toward public health programs to counter addiction and educational programs to prevent it. The *National Drug Control Strategy* outlines a viable plan for addressing the US demand for illegal drugs. The specific recommendations follow:

- Strengthen efforts to prevent drug use in our communities

- Seek early intervention opportunities in health care

- Integrate treatment for substance use disorders into mainstream health care and expand support for recovery

- Break the cycle of drug use, crime, delinquency, and incarceration

- Disrupt domestic drug trafficking and production

- Strengthen international partnerships

- Improve information systems for analysis, assessment and local management[79]

The *National Drug Control Strategy* further states that "we must also stop the illicit flow from the United States of weapons and criminal proceeds that empower TOC networks."[80] It emphasizes additional resources and capabilities for the integrated Border Enforcement Security Task Forces on our southern border "to investigate the organizations involved in cross-border crimes."[81] What is perhaps the most telling aspect of the *Drug Control Strategy* is that the Department of Defense is mentioned only once in the entire document.

"Only the Defense Department is able to do that," is an oft-used excuse for other US Government departments relying on DoD resources, rather than those departments obtaining and maintaining their own capabilities. The Drug Enforcement Administration and the Federal Bureau of Investigation (FBI) should pursue adequate funding from Congress to fully support their missions, to alleviate and end their dependence on DoD for transportation, reconnaissance, and other support functions. Congress should also adequately fund the Department of Homeland Security (DHS) and LEAs to control our borders. They must have the technical capabilities to conduct successful intelligence, surveillance and reconnaissance missions and have sufficient funding to hire more personnel to apprehend persons entering the US illegally, especially since they could be trafficking in illegal substance or be the victims of human trafficking. LEA intelligence units should be adequately resourced to monitor and stop the flow of weapons from the US to Latin American cartels, and to track cartel finances where possible.

Rather than compelling DoD to continue or become further immersed in a fight it has not been able to win, perhaps the time has come to reallocate those resources to law enforcement agencies and allow the Department to reprioritize its core missions, especially given today's budget cuts and associated downsizing. Being good stewards of taxpayers' money demands that DoD dedicate its precious resources to where it can best accomplish mission. At a time when the military is in the midst of an effort to rearm, train and refit itself to perform its key missions, and with dramatically reduced resources, those programs showing the least success and the least relevance to core missions should at least be closely scrutinized.

On January 26, 2012 the Department issued its plan to cut more than $259 billion during FY13-17.[82] Since the Congressional Super Committee failed to reach the hoped for compromise on US Government spending cuts, DoD is obligated to prepare for even deeper cuts than previously projected, and perhaps, sequestration. At a time when the Department is refocusing on its key mission areas and considering dropping non-critical missions, this author submits that the time to reconsider the continued viability of DoD's counternarcotics mission has come. The less than two billion dollar DoD counternarcotics budget is a small percentage of the Department's overall budget, reflecting its low level of significance vis-à-vis the overall DoD mission. In time of declining budgets the Defense Department should not be performing ancillary missions, and should instead focus on key threats to best protect our national security.

The new *National Defense Strategy* identifies the key military missions for which DoD must prepare. Specifically, those missions are: counterterrorism and irregular warfare, to deter and defeat aggression, power projection, counter weapons of mass destruction, operate effectively in space and cyberspace, maintain the nuclear deterrent, defend the homeland the provide support to civil authorities, provide a stabilizing presence (abroad), conduct stability and counterinsurgency operations, conduct humanitarian disaster relief and other operations.[83] Let the US military conduct the missions it is best trained and equipped to perform, - those identified above. The DoD should not be treated as a contractor with services available for hire to other departments. It should perform missions that it is uniquely capable of performing, not additional missions it is *able* to perform or support. DoD's resources are greatly constrained. The Department needs to be prepared for the next 9/11 and other crises. It does not need to be performing ancillary missions, especially those for which there has been so little return on more than two decades of investment.

Should analysts one day identify a clear sustained link between drug cartels and terrorist organizations, the US Government would need to determine how to best address that threat, and if it constituted a national security threat to the US. Obviously if such a nexus appeared to threaten a government deemed hostile to US interests, Washington would probably choose to monitor the situation from afar. Also, if the nexus proved to be a one-time localized linkage the US' concern would be less than if such a nexus seemed to be a model that other criminal and terrorist organizations had reason to follow. If cartels and terrorist organizations came together in a way deemed a serious credible threat to US national security interests, the services of the US Armed Forces could and should be called upon to meet it. Even then, the military should only be called upon if given a clear strategy for success, achievable end states, and an exit strategy.

Endnotes

[1] George H.W. Bush, "Speech Before Joint Session of Congress," The Capitol, Washington, DC, February 9, 1989, http://millercenter.org/president/speeches/detail/3420 (accessed March 25, 2012).

[2] Government Accountability Office (GAO), *Drug Control: Status Report on DoD Support to Counternarcotics Activities* (Washington, DC: US Government Acountability Office, June 1991), 4.

[3] Donald Mabry, "The US Military and the War on Drugs in Latin America," *Journal of Interamerican Studies and World Affairs*, 30, no. 2/3 (Summer 1988): 57.

[4] Peter Zirnite, "Reluctant Recruits – The US Military and the War on Drugs," *Washington Office on Latin America*, August 1997: Washington, DC http://www.tni.org/sites/www.tni.org/files/download/Reluctant%20recruits%20report_0.pdf (accessed March 31, 2012).

[5] George H.W. Bush, National Security Directive 18 (NSD 18), *International Counternarcotics Strategy*, (Washington, DC: The White House, August 21, 1989), 1.

[6] GAO, 12.

[7] Peter Zirnite, *Reluctant Recruits.*

[8] Bush, *NSD 18*, 2-3.

[9] US Secretary of State James Baker, "Guidance on General Thurman's Visit," cable for US Andean embassies, Washington, DC, October 3, 1989 (DTG 030025Z Oct 89).

[10] "Pentagon Expands Mission of Military," *St. Louis Post-Dispatch*, September 19, 1989.

[11] Ed Vulliamy, "Nixon's War on Drugs Began 40 Years Ago, and the Battle is Still Raging," *The Observer*, July 23, 2011 http://www.guardian.co.uk/society/2011/jul/24/war-on-drugs-40-years (accessed March 10, 2012).

[12] MAJ Craig T. Trebelcock, USAR, "The Myth of Posse Comitatus," October 2000, http://www.homelandsecurity.org/journal/articles/trebilcock.htm (accessed January 9, 2012).

[13] Brig Gen John S. Brown, US Army Retired, "Historically Speaking: Border Security," *Army* (December 2007): 86.

[14] US Code Title 10, Chapter 18, Sections 371 – 373, http://www.law.cornell.edu/uscode/text/10/subtitle-A/part-I/chapter-18 (accessed November 9, 2011 and March 29, 2012).

[15] Mabry, "The US Military," 53.

[16] Zirnite, "Reluctant Recruits."

[17] David "Perera, "Cost of Military Deployments along the Southwestern Border Depend on Legal Authority, says GAO," FierceHomelandSecurity.com, http://www.fiercehomelandsecurity.com/story/cost-military-deployments-along-southwestern-border-depend-legal-authority-/2011-09-12 (accessed on January 28, 2012).

[18] Brown, "Historically Speaking," 85.

[19] Douglas Stanglin, "Planes, Helos to Replace Guardsmen on Border," *Army Times.* http://www.armytimes.com/news/2011/12/gannett-planes-helos-to-replace-guardsmen-border-122111/ (accessed on January 28, 2012).

[20] Aliya Sternstein, "Military Surveillance Planes will Begin Patrolling the Southwest Border in January," *Nextgov.com*, December 20, 2011, http://www.nextgov.com/nextgov/ng_20111220_8137.php (accessed on January 28, 2012).

[21] Douglas Stanglin, "Planes, Helos to Replace Guardsmen on Border," *Army Times.* http://www.armytimes.com/news/2011/12/gannett-planes-helos-to-replace-guardsmen-border-122111/ (accessed on January 28, 2012).

[22] "Pentagon Weighs Use of Military on the Border," *Security on MSNBC.com*, http://www.msnbc.msn.com/id/12748088/ns/us_news-security/t/pentagon-weighs-use-military-border/ (accessed March 20, 2012); Patrick Brady, "The Military and Border Security,"

Military.com, http://www.military.com/opinion/0,15202,214573,00.html (accessed March 20, 2012).

[23] "Rick Perry Suggests US Military Role in Mexico Drug War," *BBC News,* October 1, 2011, http://www.bbc.co.uk/news/world-latin-america-15140560 (accessed March 25, 2012).

[24] US Senators John McCain and Jon Kyl, "McCain, Kyl Announce Border Security Plan, 10-Point Plan to Better Secure the US-Mexico Border in Arizona," press release, April 19, 2010 http://mccain.senate.gov/public/index.cfm?FuseAction=PressOffice.PressReleases&ContentRe cord_id=18459278-ac95-e53d-0c3a-427b2010565f&Region_id=&Issue_id= (accessed March 24, 2012).

[25] Sam Howe Verhovek, "No Charges Against Marine in Border Killing," *The New York Times,* August 15, 1997, http://www.nytimes.com/1997/08/15/us/no-charges-against-marine-in-border-killing.html (accessed November 15, 2011).

[26] Deputy Assistant Secretary of Defense for Counternarcotics and Global Threats (DASD CN&GT), Special Operations/Low Intensity Conflict, Office of the Undersecretary of Defense for Policy, "DoD Counternarcotics Program" briefing slides, Washington, DC, November 2011.

[27] Ibid.

[28] William R. Brownfield, *Is Merida Antiquated? Part Two: Updating U.S. Policy to Counter Threats of Insurgency and Narco-Terrorism,* House Foreign Affairs Subcommittee on the Western Hemisphere and House Homeland Security Subcommittee on Oversight, Investigations and Management, October 4, 2011, Internet. http://www.state.gov/j/inl/rls/rm/175007.htm (accessed November 16, 2011).

[29] "Mexico: Organised Crime Fight Drives Backlash," *OxResearch Daily Brief Service.* Oxford, UK, August 2, 2011, 1.

[30] *The New York Times,* "Mexican Drug Trafficking," January 19, 2012, http://topics.nytimes.com/top/news/international/countriesandterritories/mexico/drug_trafficking/i ndex.html (accessed March 24, 2012).

[31] "One Killed Every Half Hour in Mexico Drug-Related Violence," *MSNBC.com,* January 12, 2012, http://worldnews.msnbc.msn.com/_news/2012/01/12/10138166-one-killed-every-half-hour-in-mexico-drug-related-violence (accessed March 24, 2012).

[32] Ibid.

[33] Barack Obama, *2011 National Drug Control Strategy* (Washington, DC: The White House, 2011), http://www.whitehouse.gov/ondcp/ chapter-strengthen-international-partnerships#1 (accessed March 12, 2012).

[34] Juan Carlos Llorca and Frank Bajak, "Mexican Drug Cartels Expand Abroad," *Associated Press,* July 21, 2009 http://www.blnz.com/news/2009/07/21/IMPACT_Mexican_drug_cartels_ expand_1137.html (accessed March 24, 2012).

[35] Bush, NSD 18, 2.

[36] Eva Bertram, Morris Blachman, Kenneth Sharpe, and Peter Andreas, *Drug War Politics: The Price of Denial* (Berkeley, California: University of California Press, 1996), 13.

[37] Ibid.

[38] James Q. Roberts, Principal Director for Special Operations and Counterterrorism, Special Operations/Low Intensity Conflict, Office of the Undersecretary of Defense for Policy, interview by author, Arlington, VA, November 23, 2011.

[39] Ed Vulliamy, "Nixon's War on Drugs Began 40 Years Ago, and the Battle is Still Raging," *The Observer*, July 23, 2011 http://www.guardian.co.uk/society/2011/jul/24/war-on-drugs-40-years (accessed March 10, 2012).

[40] Government Accountability Office (GAO), "Drug Control: DoD Needs to Improve its Performance Measurement System to Better Manage and Oversee Its Counternarcotics Activities," *Report to Congressional Committees*, (Washington, DC: GAO, July 2010), 35.

[41] Deputy Assistant Secretary of Defense for Counternarcotics and Global Threats, *DoD Counternarcotics and Global Threats Strategy*, (Washington, DC: US Department of Defense, April 27, 2011), 19.

[42] Ibid, (emphasis added).

[43] Interview with senior DoD official, November 28, 2011.

[44] Ibid.; Steven I. Taylor, "Back to the Drug War: The street Price of Cocaine," Outside the Beltway, May 16, 2010 http://www.outsidethebeltway.com/back_to_the_drug_war_the_street_price_of_cocaine/ (accessed March 6, 2012).

[45] United Nations Office on Drugs and Crime (UNODC), *World Drug Report 2011*, (New York: United Nations, 2011) http://www.unodc.org/documents/data-and-analysis/WDR2011/World_Drug_Report_2011_ebook.pdf (accessed March 9, 2012), 81.

[46] Ibid, 119.

[47] US Department of Justice National Drug Intelligence Center, *National Drug Threat Assessment 2011* (Washington, DC: US Department of Justice, August 2011), 50.

[48] Ibid.

[49] Caryn Hollis, Principal Director for Counternarcotics and Global Threats, Special Operations/Low Intensity Conflict, Office of the Undersecretary of Defense for Policy, e-mail message to author, March 28, 2012.

[50] Douglas Stanglin, "Planes, Helos to Replace Guardsmen on Border," *Army Times*. http://www.armytimes.com/news/2011/12/gannett-planes-helos-to-replace-guardsmen-border-122111/ (accessed on January 28, 2012).

[51] FY05-07 data, US House of Representatives, "The Department of Defense's Counternarcotics Efforts," Staff Report Prepared for the Honorable Mark Souder, Chairman,

Subcommittee on Criminal Justice, Drug Policy and Human Resources, December 2006, http://publicpolicypress.files.wordpress.com/2010/01/dod-counternarcotics.pdf (accessed March 24, 2012), 2; FY08-11 data, DASD CN& GT, "DoD Counternarcotics Program" briefing slides.

[52] Barack Obama, *National Security Strategy 2010* (Washington, DC: The White House, May 2010), 49.

[53] Barack Obama, *Strategy to Combat Transnational Organized Crime: Addressing Converging Threats to National Security* (Washington, DC: The White House, July 2011), 14.

[54] Leon Panetta, *Sustaining U.S. Global Leadership: Priorities for 21st Century Defense* (Washington, DC: US Department of Defense, January 2012), 5.

[55] Ibid.

[56] Ibid.

[57] Barrack Obama, "State of the Union Address," The Capitol, Washington, DC, January 24, 2012.

[58] James Clapper, "Unclassified Statement for the Record on the Worldwide Threat Assessment of the US Intelligence Community for the Senate Select Committee on Intelligence," (Washington, DC: Office of the Director of National Intelligence, January 31, 2012), 24.

[59] Ibid.

[60] Ioan Grillo, "US Troops Increase Aid to Mexico in Drug War," National Public Radio, http://www.npr.org/2011/10/06/141128178/u-s-troops-increase-aid-to-mexico-in-drug-war (accessed march 10, 2012).

[61] Roberts.

[62] Paul Rexton Kan, "What We're Getting Wrong about Mexico," *Parameters* 41, no. 2 (Summer 2011): 37.

[63] Malcolm Beith, "Are Mexico's Drug Cartels Terrorist Groups?" Slate, April 15, 2010, http://www.slate.com/articles/news_and_politics/foreigners/2010/04/are_mexicos_drug_cartels_terrorist_groups.html (accessed February 4, 2012).

[64] Maggie Ybarra and Daniel Borrunda, "Mexico Attorney General: Juarez Explosion Not Narco-terrorism," *El PasoTimes*, July 16, 2010, http://www.elpasotimes.com/ci_15531121 (accessed January 6, 2012).

[65] Kan, "What We're Getting Wrong," 38.

[66] Robert Valencia, "Mexican Drug Cartels," World Policy Blog, October 26, 2011, Accessed February 4, 2012, http://www.worldpolicy.org/blog/2011/10/26/mexican-drug-cartels-are-not-terrorists.

[67] Elizabeth Harrington, "Republicans Propose Bill to Treat Mexican Drug Cartels as 'Terrorist Insurgency,'" CNS News.com, December 15, 2011, http://cnsnews.com/news/article/republicans-propose-bill-treat-mexican-drug-cartels-terrorist-insurgency (accessed March 25, 2012).

[68] Ibid.

[69] Mike Riggs, "Cartel Involvement in Failed Iranian Assassination Plot Fuels Push for Terrorist Designation," *Reason.com*, October 21, 2011, http://reason.com/archives/2011/10/21/cartel-involvement-in-failed-i (accessed March 25, 2012).

[70] Jerry Markon and Karen DeYoung, "Iran Behind Alleged Terrorist Plot, US Says," *The Washington Post*, October 11, 2011, http://www.washingtonpost.com/world/national-security/iranian-charged-in-terror-plot/2011/10/11/gIQAiaYxcL_story.html (accessed March 25, 2012); Warren Richey, "US alleges Iranian Plot to Kill Saudi Ambassador: How It Unfolded," Christian Science Monitor, October 11, 2011, http://www.csmonitor.com/USA/Justice/2011/1011/US-alleges-Iranian-plot-to-kill-Saudi-ambassador-How-it-unfolded (accessed March 25, 2012).

[71] Valencia, "Mexican Cartels."

[72] US Department of State, "Background Note: Colombia," March 6, 2012, http://www.state.gov/r/pa/ei/bgn/35754.htm (accessed March 30, 2012).

[73] Ibid.

[74] Ibid.

[75] Deputy Assistant Secretary of Defense for Counternarcotics and Global Threats (DASD CN&GT), *DoD Counternarcotics and Global Threats Strategy*, (Washington, DC: US Department of Defense, April 27, 2011) 4.

[76] John Rollins and Liana Sun Wyler, "International Terrorism and Transnational Crime," Congressional Research Service, March 28, 2010, R41004, http://assets.opencrs.com/rpts/R41004_20100318.pdf (accessed 25 March, 2012), 6.

[77] Valencia, "Mexican Drug Cartels;" "Rick Perry," BBC.

[78] Barack Obama, *Strategy to Combat Transnational Organized Crime: Addressing Converging Threats to National Security*, (Washington, DC: The White House, July 2011) 15.

[79] Obama, *National Drug Control Strategy 2011*, i.

[80] Ibid, 15.

[81] Ibid.

[82] US Department of Defense, "Defense Budget Priorities and Choices" (Washington, DC: US Department of Defense, January 2012), 3.

[83] Leon Panetta, *Sustaining U.S. Global Leadership: Priorities for 21st Century Defense* (Washington, DC: US Department of Defense, January 2012), 4-6.